The Orphans
of
Normandy

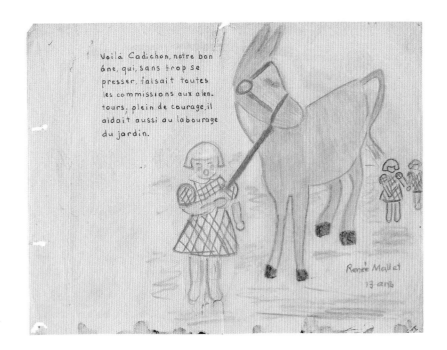

Voilà Cadichon, notre bon
âne, qui, sans trop se
presser, faisait toutes
les commissions aux alen-
tours; plein de courage, il
aidait aussi au labourage
du jardin.

Renée Mallet
13 ans

This book is for you,
Aunt Aggie, and for
the orphans of Normandy.
Love, Nancy

The Orphans
of
Normandy

A true story of World War **II**
told through drawings by children

NANCY AMIS

POCKET BOOKS

London   New York   Sydney

This edition published in 2004 by Pocket Books,
an imprint of Simon & Schuster UK Ltd
Africa House, 64-78 Kingsway, London WC2B 6AH

Originally published in 2003 by Atheneum Books for Young Readers,
an imprint of Simon & Schuster Children's Publishing Division, New York

Introduction, afterword and compilation copyright © 2003 Nancy Amis

The right of Nancy Amis to be identified as the compiler of this
work has been asserted by her in accordance with the Copyright,
Designs and Patents Act, 1988

Book designed by Ann Bobco
The text for this book is set in Granjon Bold and Blockhead Unplugged
The illustrations are rendered in coloured pencil on newsprint

A CIP catalogue record for this book is available
from the British Library upon request

ISBN 0 743 48386 3

Printed in China

1 2 3 4 5 6 7 8 9 10

acknowledgments

My great-aunt, Agnes Fulton Amis, went to France in 1919 after World War I. She knew very little French, but learned to speak the language while working among the French people. She attended the Sorbonne and later taught French as an exchange teacher to French children. Through her many friends in France, combined with the efforts of her French students and the American Relief for France, she was able to contribute to building a strong relationship between the United States and France. For her diplomatic accomplishments she was awarded in 1937, and again in 1962, the Cross of Officer from L'Ordre des Palmes Académiques.

Allons, Enfants

On June 6, 1944, one hundred girls walked silently out of their home and into the dark night. The red, white and blue tattersall dresses that they wore were their only clothes. Some of the girls had no shoes, but they had to escape from the danger of the Allied invasion of Normandy and the German defence against it.

France had been living under German occupation since 1940. The world was at war, families were split apart and many children were homeless. Before the occupation, La Maison du Clos in St. André-sur-Orne was a home and school for girls whose parents could no longer care for them or who had died. By 1944, when France was under German control, there were one hundred girls who lived at the orphanage. Before the bombs began to fall, Mademoiselle LeVallios and the teachers worked hard to provide everything the girls needed for a happy and productive life.

That night everything changed. From their bedroom window, they watched vibrant lights in the sky. Planes were flying overhead. The noise of bombs falling and machine guns rat-a-tat-ting was loud enough that they had to hold their ears closed with trembling hands.

Allons, enfants, vite, vite! We must go! Now! Hurry! Hurry! We must leave our home! *Allons, enfants.* Let's go children. Each girl carried a blanket, a little white flag and some bread. From La Maison du Clos, they walked down the driveway, through the gate and slowly, quietly, up the road and over the hill. The journey had begun.

" The Clos, on the banks of the Orne, near Caen,

welcomed little girls who were orphans without

homes, and prepared them, in a homelike

atmosphere, for life. The large estate of

twenty-five acres included . . . the residence:

kitchen, dining room, dormitories, bathrooms,

dressing rooms; the school buildings: kindergarten,

primary school, trade schools, and workrooms."

— Nicole Folliot, 13

La maison d'enfants du Clos.

(actuellement réfugiée aux Buissons. Champcueil. Seine et Oise)

Le

Clos

Situé sur

les bords de

l'Orne, près de Caen,

(actuellement réfugié aux

Vauréal par Cergy

Buissons, à Champcueil. Seine et Oise)

accueillait dès leur plus

jeune âge les petites filles sans foyer et les préparait à la vie dans une atmosphère familiale

Cette grande propriété de 9 hectares comprenait les bâtiments de la maison d'habitation : cui-

sine, réfectoires, dortoirs, lavabos, vestiaires.. les bâtiments scolaires : jardin d'enfants, écoles

Nicole Folliot
13 ans

Spring 1944

"In the schoolroom at the Clos, the little girls from three to fourteen learned their lessons."

— Emma Renad, 12

Emma Renad
12 ans

En classe, au Clos même, les petites filles de 3 à 14 ans étaient instruites.

"The more grown-up girls learned to sew, in the sunny sewing room, overlooking the river."

— Denise Lerossignal, 11

Les petites filles devenues
grandes apprenaient la cou.
ture, dans leur bel atelier
près de l'Orne.

Denise Lerossignal
11 ans

"During playtime, in the warm weather, swimming in the cool water of the Orne was wonderful. We dived all day long."

— Hélène Han, 12

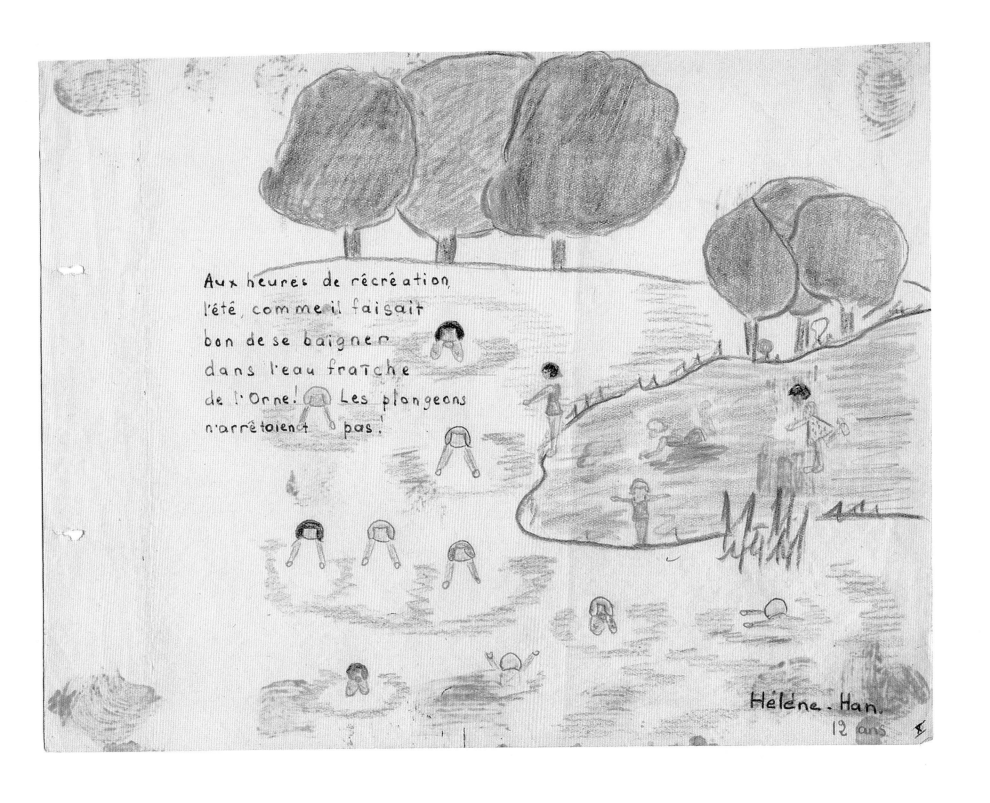

Aux heures de récréation,
l'été, comme il faisait
bon de se baigner
dans l'eau fraîche
de l'Orne! Les plongeons
n'arrêtoient pas!

Hélène. Han.
12 ans

"Gaston, the gardener of the Clos, lovingly tended the big vegetable garden, which provided us with fresh vegetables daily. Oh, the cabbage soups, the tender carrots and the juicy fruits we enjoyed!"

— Jacqueline Lacaz, 10

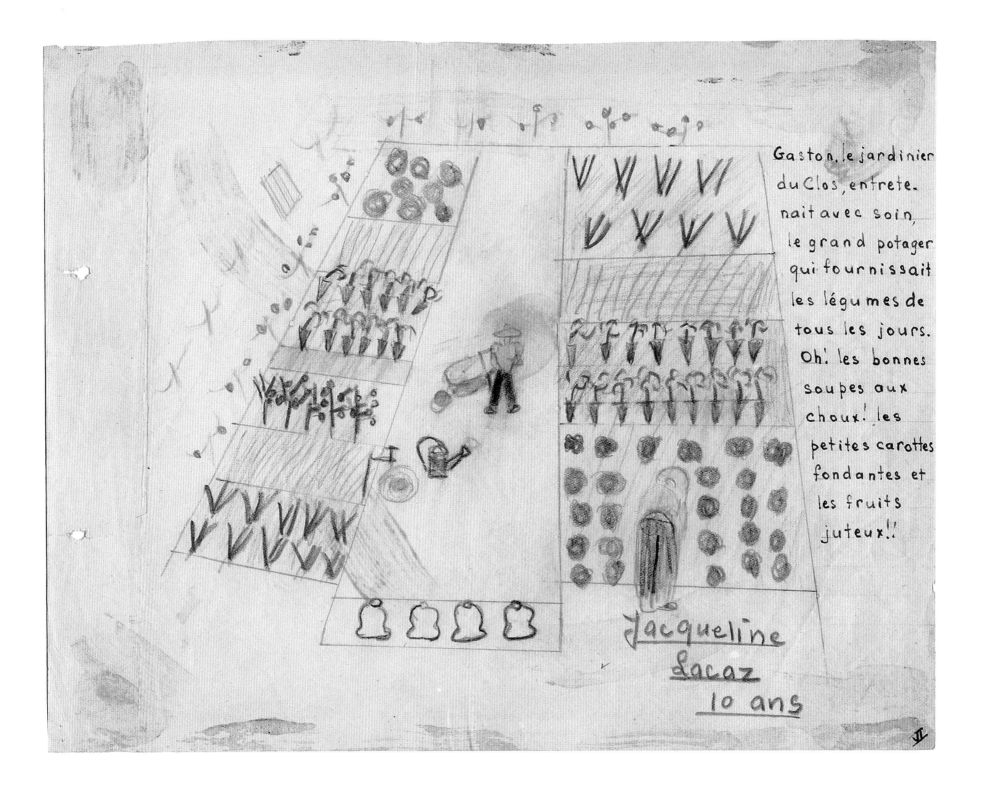

Gaston, le jardinier du Clos, entretenait avec soin, le grand potager qui fournissait les légumes de tous les jours. Oh! les bonnes soupes aux choux! les petites carottes fondantes et les fruits juteux!!

Jacqueline Lacaz 10 ans

" In an enclosure near the chicken house we had many types of fowl and a house for all our rabbits."

— Denise Fernande, 12

Dans l'enclos près du poulailler, s'ébattait une
nombreuse volaille, à laquelle se mêlaient tous
les lapins de notre clapier.

Denise Fernan de 12ans

"Under the apple trees our beautiful cows grazed.

They gave us abundant, delicious milk."

— Emma Ronquad, 12

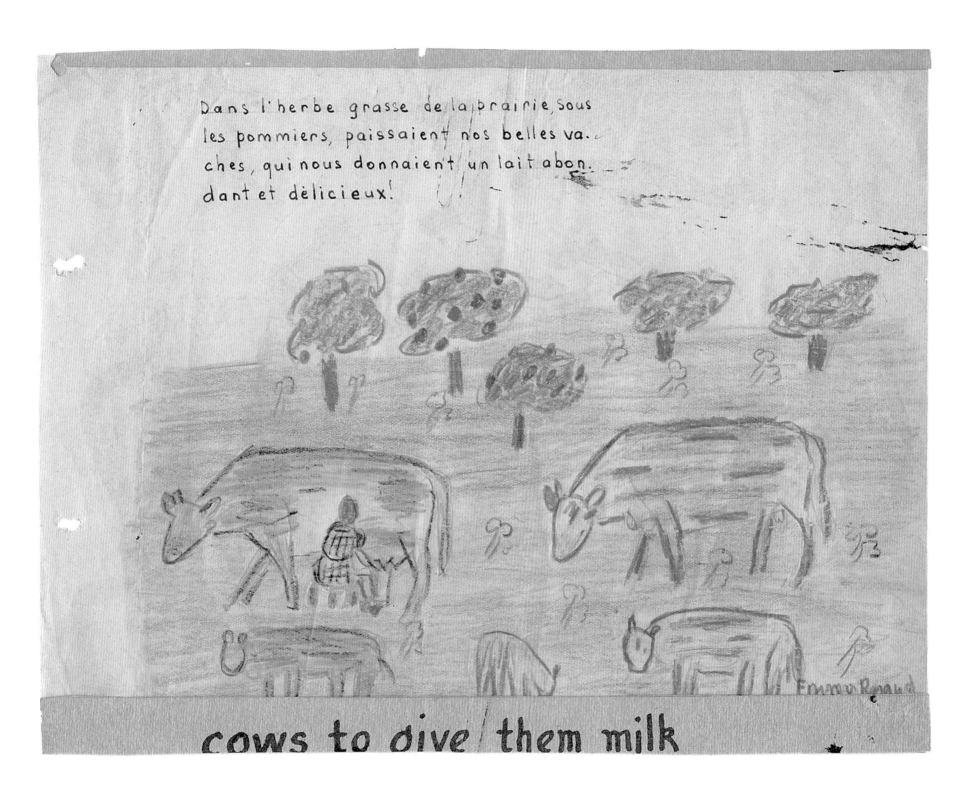

Dans l'herbe grasse de la prairie, sous les pommiers, paissaient nos belles va. ches, qui nous donnaient un lait abon. dant et délicieux!

cows to dive them milk

"The night of June 5 and 6, 1944, at the Clos, began well. Everybody went quietly to sleep as usual, but soon we were startled awake by unusual noises. The good sleepers remained, noses in pillows, but the others dashed to the windows. They listened . . . and with a sigh of relief, they shouted, 'It's the invasion!'"

— Rose Marie Vail, 12

La nuit du 5 au 6 juin 1944, au clos, commence bien: chacune s'endort tranquillement comme à l'ordinaire. Mais bientôt on se sent tiré du sommeil malgrè soi par des bruits insolites. Les bonnes dormeuses demeurent le nez plongé dans leur oreiller, mais les autres se précipitent aux fenêtres. Elles regardent le ciel...elles écoutent.. et avec un soupir de bonheur s'écrient: "C'est le... débarquement!!!

Rose Marie Vail

Rose Marie Vail
12 ans

"A half-mile from the entrance of the mine was a large space where the girls made their home. In spite of being underground there was enough air to breathe, and a little brook gave a certain amount of coolness. But it was black as night and the ground was muddy. Using firewood and straw we made our beds and here and there we hung acetylene lanterns, which were very precious in the darkness. A big wooden bench served as a table for our bread. . . . The Germans often came to search. . . . But in spite of all of the inconveniences, the little girls of the Clos felt safe in the mine where they were sheltered from the bombing."

— Monique Suret, 12

Sous la mine - A 700 mètres de l'entrée de la mine, il y a un grand espace, où toutes les petites filles s'installent. C'est tout de même assez haut pour qu'on puisse y respirer, et un petit ruisseau y entretient une certaine fraîcheur. Mais il y fait nuit et le sol est boueux! A l'aide de fagots de bois et de bottes de paille, on confectionne les lits, et de place en place on suspend une lampe à carbure, si précieuse dans notre obscurité. Un grand banc servira de table pour poser le pain... Ici, il faut tenir le moins de place possible, et demeurer assis plutôt que debout. Très souvent on attendra longtemps le ravitaillement qui ne pourra arriver à cause des obus pleuvant au dehors. Les Allemands viendront faire des fouilles. Mais malgré toutes ces incommodités, les petites filles du clos sont rassurées d'être sous la mine, où elles sont à l'abri des bombardements.

Monique Suret
12 ans

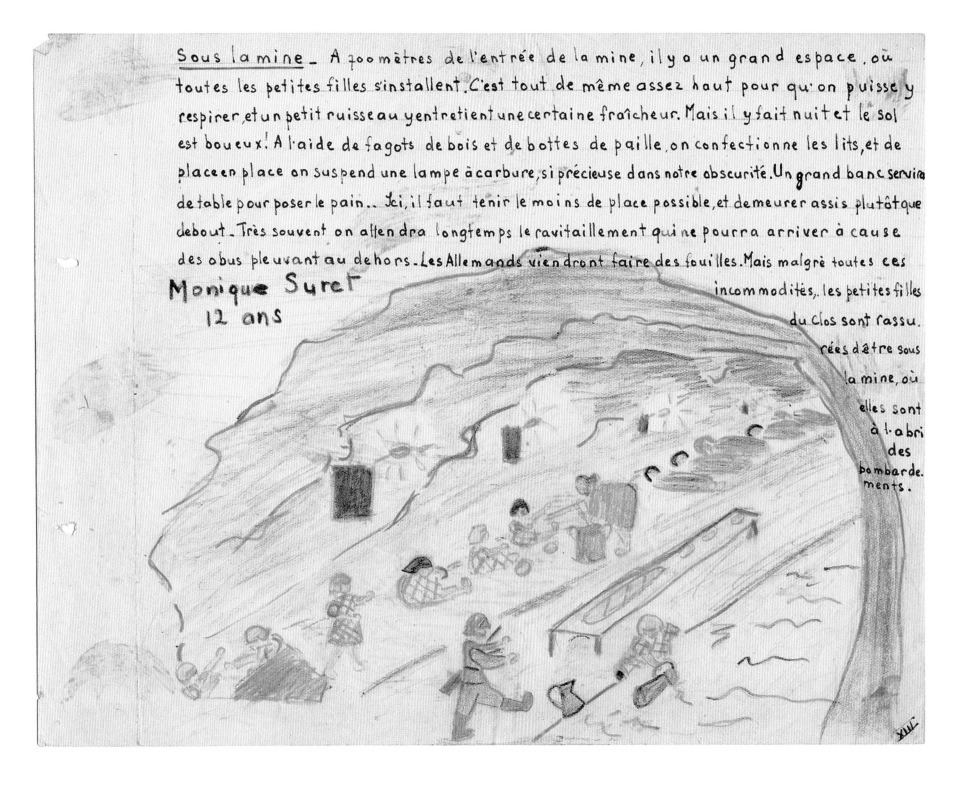

XVII

"Back in the Clos, which was all but abandoned, the Germans stole and ate our poor little rabbits."

— Mauricette Bourdin, 10

Dans le Clos presque aban-
donné, les Allemands volent
et mangent nos pauvres pe-
tits lapins!

Mounette Bourdin
10 ans

"In the beginning of July a plane dived and bombed German trucks hidden near the Clos. Some Germans were killed; others wounded . . . the truck burned . . . and our poor mill also. . . . The Clos's two automobiles parked nearby burned too."

— Jeannine Ollichon, 12

Jeannine Ollichon
12 ans

Au début de Juillet un avion pique et bombarde
la roulante allemande réfugiée près du Clos _ Des Alle.
mands sont tués, d'autres blessés.. la roulante flambe .. et
notre pauvre moulin aussi! Il n'y a donc plus d'ateliers au clos!
Les deux autos du clos garées près de là ont brûlé aussi!

"July **14**. The Germans made the little girls of the Clos evacuate the mine. With no destination they took to the road . . . beneath the planes . . . under the shells. . . . Cadichon, our donkey, hauled the littlest ones who were too small to walk long distances."

— Nicole Folliot, 13

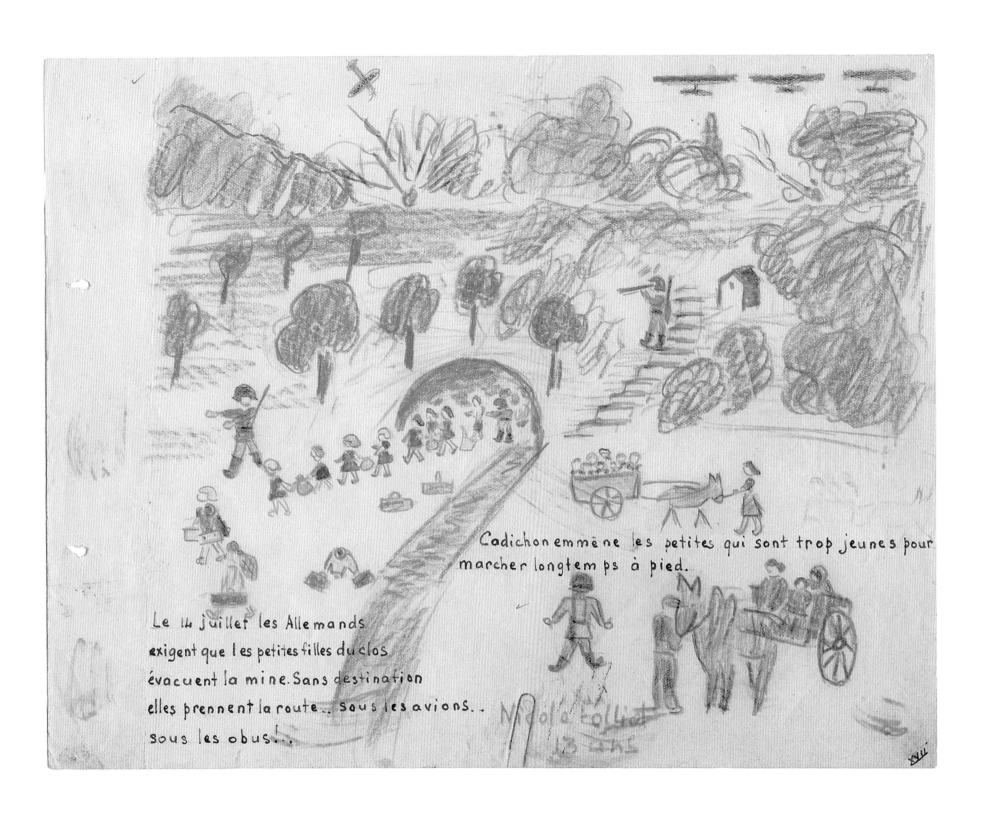

Cadichon emmène les petites qui sont trop jeunes pour marcher longtemps à pied.

Le 14 juillet les Allemands exigent que les petites filles du clos évacuent la mine. Sans destination elles prennent la route.. sous les avions.. sous les obus!..

Nicole Colliet
13 ans

"Crossing the Cinglais forest, the girls passed German tanks in flames and dead Germans. The brave little girls of the Clos followed other evacuees. All the while waving their white flags at the approaching planes."

— Odette Daigromont, 13

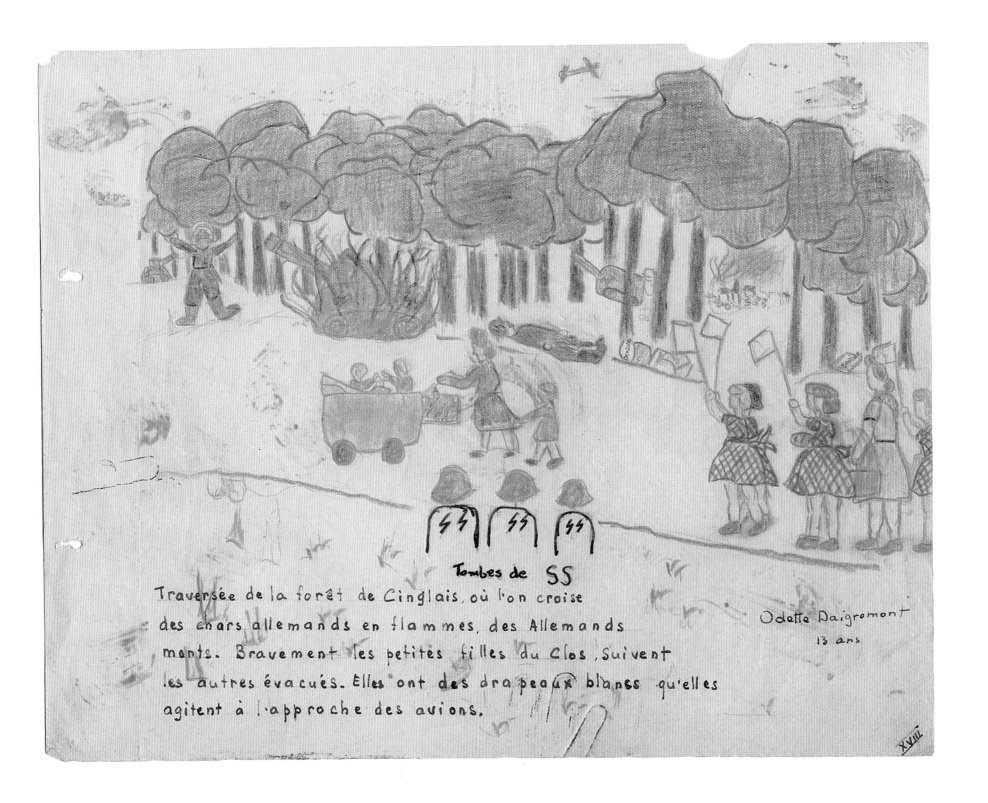

Tombes de SS

Traversée de la forêt de Cinglais, où l'on croise
des chars allemands en flammes, des Allemands
morts. Bravement les petites filles du Clos, suivent
les autres évacués. Elles ont des drapeaux blancs qu'elles
agitent à l'approche des avions.

Odette Daigremont
13 ans

XVIII

"July 15. We stopped at Acqueville in order to rest and regain our strength. As we ate lunch under the apple trees two American planes dived low and then, seeing us, climbed quickly and machine-gunned the road a little farther on. We finished our lunch with hearty appetites under the terrified eyes of the Germans."

— Yvonne Rognant, 11

Yvonne Rognant
11 ans

15 Juillet : stationnement à Acqueville afin de
reprendre des forces. Mais le déjeuner sous les pommiers
est troublé par deux avions qui piquent bas. et qui, nous voyant sans
doute remontent vite, et vont mitrailler la route un peu plus loin. On termine le
repas de bon appétit sous l'oeil apeuré des Allemands.

"July 19. We went through Falaise silent but filled with emotion. We had to go single file through the streets. The girls of the Clos were astounded to see such ruins. The Germans had been driven out."

— Marcelle Blavier, 14

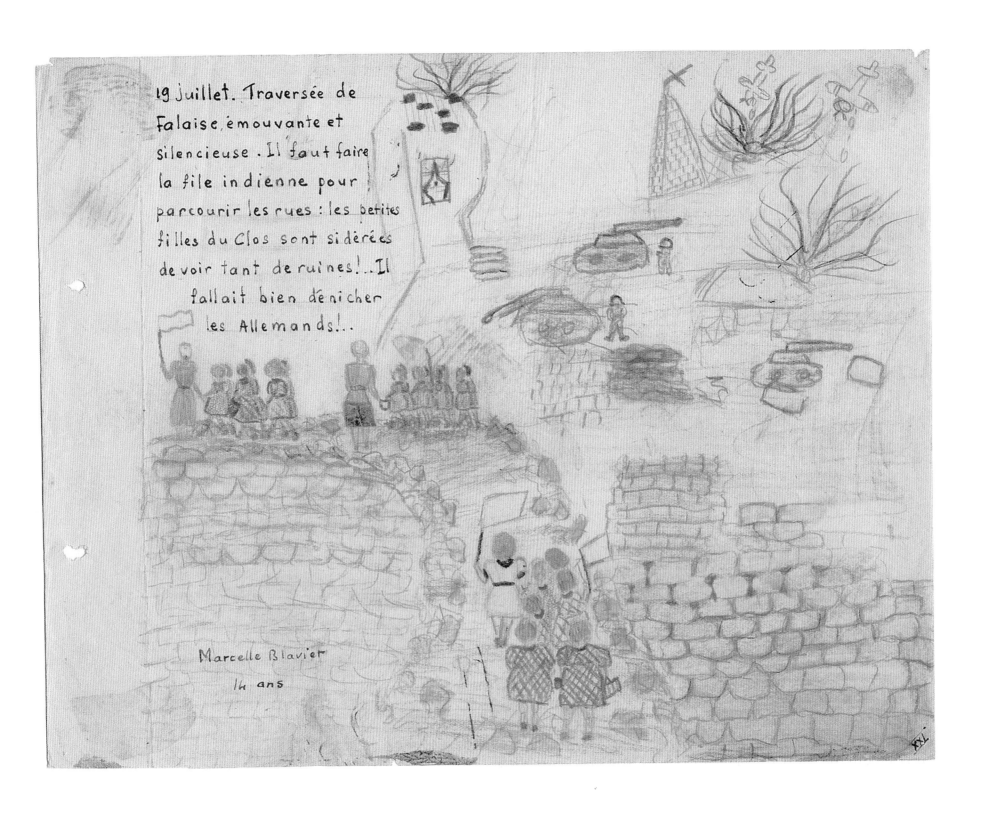

19 Juillet. Traversée de Falaise, émouvante et silencieuse. Il faut faire la file indienne pour parcourir les rues : les petites filles du Clos sont sidérées de voir tant de ruines!... Il fallait bien dénicher les Allemands!...

Marcelle Blavier
14 ans

"July 23. On the way to Argentan, whose spires we saw in the distance. More planes were on the prowl. . . . A convoy of British prisoners passed and the little girls made signs to show they were friends. The planes dived but climbed again very quickly, realising we were a friendly group of little girls in pink dresses waving our flags, but with a little shiver of fear up and down our spines."

— Jeannette Renaud, 13

Jeannette Renoud
13 ans

23 Juillet. En route vers Argentan dont on distingue au
loin les clochers! Les avions rôdent. les voilà qui arrivent vers nous.
En même temps passe sur la route un convoi de prisonniers anglais aux-
quels les petites filles font quelques signes d'amitié _ Les avions piquent, mais
remontent bien vite, se rendant compte qu'ils ont à faire à des compatriotes
et à un groupe de petites filles en rose agitant bien leurs drapeaux ... avec
tout de même un petit frisson de peur dans le dos.

"July 29. Now travelling in farmers' carts, the little girls of the Clos make a short stop at St. Suzanne, a picturesque little village where they are received kindly by everybody. The littlest ones joyfully drink the sweet milk served to them by order of the mayor."

— Jeannette Renaud, 13

Jeannette
13 ans Renaud

29 Juillet. Amenées en charrettes, les petites
filles du Clos, font une courte halte à Ste Suzanne,
petite ville pittoresque où elles sont reçues gentiment par
tout le monde. Les plus petites boivent avec joie le bon lait
que le maire fait servir.

"Sometimes the little girls of the Clos slept in the welcome shelter of haylofts and haystacks, thanks to the farmers. We were glad to stretch out and sleep in the cool hay."

— Denise Fernande, 12

Au hasard des étapes, les greniers des fermes accueillantes, abritent le sommeil des petites filles du Clos..qui s'étendaient avec plaisir dans la paille fraîche.

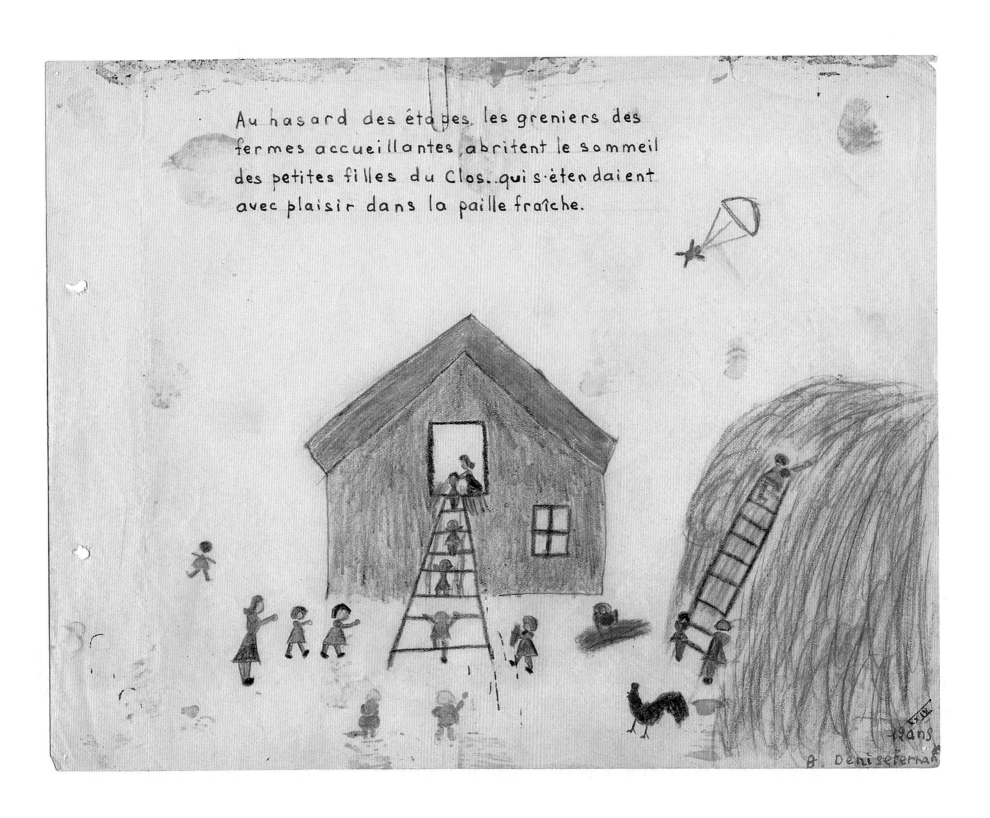

"All the way to end of their exodus, the little girls of the Clos waved their flags. They arrived at Beaufort, the end of their long trip, all safe and sound."

— Jacqueline Lacaze, 10

Jusqu'à la fin de leur exode les petites filles du clos agiteront leurs drapeaux. Elles arrivent, à Beaufort, terme de leur long voyage, toutes saines et sauves!

Jacqueline Lacaze 10 ans

"August 11. A few days after their arrival at Beaufort, the little girls of the Clos were happy to see American tanks. That consoled them for all that they had lost."

— Artist unknown

11 Août. Quelques jours après leur arrivée à Beaufort, les petites filles du Clos, ont le bonheur de voir arriver les tanks américains! Cela les console de tout ce qu'elles ont perdu!

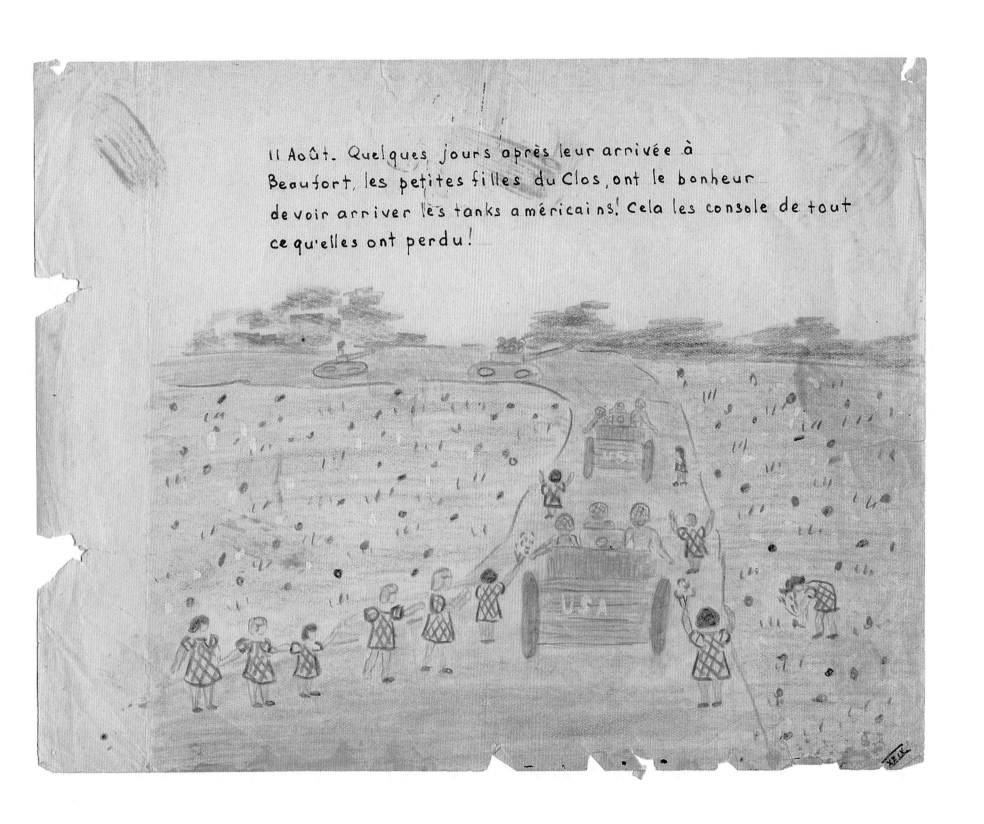

Afterword

Over a gentle hill, down a tree-lined country road and through the open gates of a long stone wall La Maison de Clos still stands just outside of the village of St. André-sur-Orne. At the end of a short drive, you will see a large yellow stone house, which sits on the banks of the Orne River. Today the apple trees are overgrown and the water mill is a single ivy covered wall. Someone still cares for the garden. Le Clos is no longer a home for girls.

Moving from one place to another became a way of life for the orphans from St. André-sur-Orne. By 1946 they found a permanent home at Le Clos de Vaureal, a fifteenth-century chateau on the Oise River, north of Paris. The buildings and grounds were perfect for a new orphanage. But how could they pay for it? The girls were without shoes. They wore bedroom slippers because they were easy to find. They did not have beds to sleep on, so they slept on pallets stuffed with dry grass and without sheets or woollen blankets.

In 1946 Agnes Amis, a French teacher in America, received a package from her friend, Yvonne Lescure, the directress of a school in Caen, France. In the package Miss Amis found

Yvonne Lescure and Agnes Amis in 1962

photographs of children; a small child's dress; and an illustrated journal with drawings of a large house, a garden and a donkey. Miss Amis quickly responded to the letter from Mme. Lescure and care packages from America began to arrive at the new orphanage. Years later I sat on a small bed next to my great-aunt Aggie. She read from a journal about a war, a journey and little girls from Normandy, while I carefully turned each page.

The site of the orphanage today as seen in this photo taken in 2000

La maison d'enfants du Clos.

(actuellement réfugiée aux Buissons, Champcueil, Seine et Oise)

Le
Clos
Situé sur
les bords de
l'Orne, près de Caen
(actuellement réfugié aux
Buissons, à Champcueil, Seine et Oise)
accueillait dès leur plus

jeune âge les petites filles sans foyer et les préparait à la vie dans une atmosphère familiale
Cette grande propriété de 9 hectares comprenait les bâtiments de la maison d'habitation : cuisine, réfectoires, dortoirs, lavabos, vestiaires … les bâtiments scolaires : jardin d'enfants, écoles

Spring 1944

A drawing of the orphanage by Nicole Folliot, 13

Clos de Vaureal

The orphans in Vaureal, France

Group photo of the orphans taken in Vaureal, France